A Theory for What Just Happened

_____

Laurie Blauner

FUTURECYCLE PRESS
www.futurecycle.org

Cover artwork, *From Generation to Generation IV* (detail), by Nancy Current; author photo by Dave Dintenfass; cover and interior book design by Diane Kistner; Georgia text with ITC Legacy Sans titling

Library of Congress Control Number: 2020947247

Published by FutureCycle Press
Athens, Georgia, USA

ISBN 978-1-952593-12-3

Contents

SHY INSTRUMENTS
OF MISUNDERSTANDING

PERSONAL CATASTROPHIC

STILL LIFE
WITH NERVOUS ANIMALS

SHY INSTRUMENTS
OF MISUNDERSTANDING

I Am That Thing

Somewhere a woman is being told she's not like the others,
or some version of it. Question: is it accidental?
Answer: everything is a rehearsal. She is developing
outside her head. She does her best to have second thoughts.
She has a grown-up manner. The woman tells me she does things
on purpose like buying furniture too big for her rooms
or mixing up rain and snoring. But I am already too old
for her and I don't know where she hides her heart.
I am the book interrupted during all hours
and in the best parts. I am hair that rises and must see things
for itself. The woman realizes that she's not special,
then sells herself short. I am what she sells.
I hold my breath to make the moment last longer.
I don't worry. I am like everyone else. I speak my mind.

A Crack in Everything Else

The forest that crawls between us is tattered and rotting.
Behind leaves, firmly in place, bones of light
nuzzle my skin. *You are an instrument,* I tell these glass walls.
I carry a haphazard suitcase. I seek beauty.

Everyone watches but no one approaches, the fence littered
with broken men. Only the bloodless evening argues with
my father, the king. (I can't leave either.) I was beside
the moon, my door opening onto a muscular field.

A bird flies against the turrets. *Leave me alone,* I scream
at all the people. They smile inside. *You see the mechanism
of the world,* my father explains. But too much is clear,
all that incongruent understanding, an untethered fern,

a horse, sacrifice. I can't touch myself
without thinking about moss or unopened flowers.
I grow political, waiting for people with wings to fall
finally inside the glass. You believe nothing terrible

can happen. I echo aberrantly. My wishes scratch
walls, trying to escape. I am becoming myself. A downtrodden
landscape between us withers. Father says,
You have learned to care for others. Now come to me.

Day of Nothing Else

Inside I tried to pick a side,
stay with it, while you decided what
you were doing. This was
someone else's house.

You were the biggest part of our dark life,
a name attached to the darkest face there.
Don't stop. Don't forget me here.
I believed in that word over there,
the one caught between your fingers,
something valuable for the taking.

I was laughing, knowing what we did. Outside,
distant streets, birds pretending to be angels.
Ideas disguised as dreams were pressed against
these windows, looking in. Afternoon climbed
in with its ugly, little feet. You sighed,
belief on both sides of you.

The owners couldn't find the pleasure
I left behind, the ceiling in my throat, the corners
creasing our skin. Who entered? Who exited?
Even my hair, draped across your shoulders, took nothing
for granted. *Try and find the body hidden here.*

Anonymous

I am what I was, everyone in Florida
with calamitous horses and their shadows.

I bought a mare and she puffs displeasure.
My friends are certain I listen. I take the stairs.

I've been promised papers that explain how
abbreviated animals have ruined one another.

Everyone is harmless until they're overrun
by the couples I let change me.

My friends ride their obedience. I don't understand.
The animals depart yet I am benign.

Anonymity ends with horses cranking our heads
back into place, recanting sparrows on all sides,

waiting. Nothing is the same. I tell the couples
about the crow tattooed on my thigh. They just laugh.

I'm not sure what that kind of humor means but
I grow suspicious with all those wings across my face.

Pillow

All day blossoms fuss,
the sky a vestibule of visible clouds.
Night echoes. I lie down in a variable

darkness that tickles my nose like a missing dog.
Whose house is it? I rearrange a fuchsia,
disorder an outrageous star. Who says I can't love

strangers? These art deco glasses remind me that blackness
still succumbs to the ludicrous moon with her face
pressed to the window. Our buttons smile at us from

your bedroom floor. Again. Afterwards
my throat is a pillow. I reach into the lamplight and
steady the remaining night. Small dreams

churn until morning. I can't see what's out there,
a comet blind to my needs or the unspooling of trees
in wind, touches that billow through me. I awaken,

turn to the body that's not mine and whisper *farewell.*
Done with my restless hand, I accommodate
yours, my hips returned like a present.

Old-Fashioned about What Went before Me

We stopped to fasten you
to seams my hair whisked through.
You were attached to something
I didn't want any part of, an unaltered past.
My hands shuffled dirt in my garden,
which was all roses, hurt stomachs, tomatoes,
no mouths yet. I spoke. All you heard were words
swinging your body back and forth. A landscape
listened from the outside, offering us redundant
domestic animals and overstuffed plants, none
of which were either yours or mine. I admitted being
partial towards fur, its elegance and warmth
reminiscent of travel. How we needed
camouflage, convexing ourselves
until time and place could work within
weather. What's a girl to do with
her unbridled imagination but expand herself
until she possesses the world and
there's nowhere else to go except backwards?

Rocket Science

July 20, 1969

Blind men checked cramped, gray rocks,
flames singeing flesh from bone,
the velocity of happiness, the dreams of contraptions
it had all come down to. We couldn't go any further.
Fistfuls of stars bumbled by.

The unseen swore deceptively.
We couldn't say much with our shallow lungs,
sky falling into preordained sectors.
We saw a dazzling brightness, tried it on slowly,
until nothing worked. We tried again,
breathing into a window that held the Earth.

We sped through everything: ghostly messages,
wind that stepped everywhere recklessly,
lines that tethered and unbound us, our lives.
We had to dance before we could touch anything useful.
Air tied us together.

A man folded down and a world arrived.

Where I Lost Myself

I seemed to know what I was doing
that morning, with all those available surfaces,
until stray dogs appeared. What did they tell
you? The moon dispensed light everywhere,
without invitation. In that personal light
you always took the same shape. I couldn't talk myself
into caring, although I tried. Disentanglement was
just about right. Danger aimed itself at me until
I fell apart. Well, so much for engagement.
So much for nature shoveling all the good parts
to exposed ground. I wanted yellow shoes.
Those clunky things fell from the sky,
making a racket among the scenery. You, too, were
laughing among the shrubs. Night was running
late. I didn't understand what couldn't be given up
or that what I got myself into was the beginning
of our skittish ghosts. I amassed moments planted
near trees. Your shoes hurt my smaller feet.

No one cares about mistakes except
the people who are them.

Our voices collected in the leaves.
Flowers grew right through us. You'd think
they could find us in the reckless dust,
with all its squirming and curiosity.
I don't know if I make sense anymore
with all that unfixed air, that desire to be found again.

Learning a Thing or Two

I wanted to entertain my body.

No one was waiting. No one could see me.

Or so I thought, a spine of my sheet in motion.

Glued to night, I imagined boys flanking me as if I were a horse.

I knew my mouth was expecting something.

There were witnesses everywhere: windows

aimed at me thoughtlessly after all those dreams.

I couldn't deny the faces or the dog that barked

its misunderstandings. My body mirrored theirs.

Once I wanted to be good enough.

I'll leave wet parts behind, hoping that

what doesn't return has already escaped.

Anywhere, Strategy #3

I threw myself into clothes waving
like flags until they, too, grew bored.
School, washing, eating until life climbed from

my room again and again. I had wanted to adorn
this town. I resisted as long as I could—
shadows moved north sending back messages

that tore right through us like clouds.
I got emotional. I rushed where there was a need,
yet I didn't want to change anything.

Now we're moving again, our fingers small boats,
tapping. Next summer will look like a surly girl
on a fence with a moon that makes everything worse.

Night calls me to the window. Your pickup stumbles
against our silence on its way out. Our families
bucketed back and forth between us. There's an address

inside your body. I'll go where I'm needed.
At the end of the road I'll meet my former selves.
We'll leave one of them outside, shivering, inside out.

Love Poem with Too Many Distractions

I was ornithologically
yours
     before I knew it
small manufactured bone
   from the body's revolutions
   whirred
with unresolved feelings
I said nothing
     and still I was in
the wrong place
    time
   for ghostly couples
in flight
    believing life
was never like that

We climbed
     back into ourselves
   adjusted
our breathing
    effacement
   with too many surfaces
abandoned
     our feathery bodies
   where they fell
   widening
my dress filled with birds
   I disappeared
   you understood
turbulence at home
    unprotected
a branch dreaming of leaves
   under a sky
that won't be the same
    again

Don't Take This the Wrong Way

There's something to be said about
looking in the mirror with a pair of upraised
scissors in your hand. It proves nothing except
that you were in the airport, flying into light.
Doors full of guesses were shaking in the sky.
Words were bitten from the middle.
What can't be admitted will be floating in air.

A girl with braids was dreaming of dolls
with bees escaping from their painted lips.
A man in a white shirt waved, believing he knew you.
We needed to keep them out of the way.

Down the aisle our inventions rose, peered out windows,
discussed a new city. Our small pleasures were over,
an erroneous landscape, one of ice and buildings
that happened often. The best parts were
our mistakes and a complicated explanation of buttons.

Let's pretend that we've landed in the right country with
our messy mouths and wind blowing through our hair.
We'll send our better selves outside
to reconnoiter this foreign world that could easily
erase us with one fearful cut. I imagined this
was where we would arrive. Nothing could be our fault.

Target Practice

I was pointing in all directions.

Everything was wrong, in case you asked.

We picked a moment

with a noticeable center
to surprise us. We knew the rest because

what had we learned about silence?

The worst part grew on us,
fumbling with our buttons, our zippers.

We were stuck.

Families moved as far away as they could.

I was broken, tumbling with wind.

Even surrounding you, I never believed
you'd fill me.

There was no end to our beginning...

everyone grew smaller, further.

You didn't see me arrive,

as if there was more to come,
as if we liked what we were doing.

How Are You, Hypothetically?

I knew him from the outside. Right or wrong.

His eye went elsewhere, nibbling at what occurred in the world.

Our conversation: chewing the impossible; resembling a window;

imagining everything; forgetting itself. We were left here.

What was wearing him? We talked around

the brutality of fences, unlikely tools, wreckage.

I was rusting inside. I was still full of birds and small animals.

He railed about After-the-Fact. We gathered architecture,

opened to—I didn't know what or whom. Skeletons poked

at the ground. A soundless horse at the top of some stairs,

ran as it could. Leaves stained red with blood. A lullaby

from a box couldn't cure us although it tried.

We found water for a reason. I was armed and ready

with nothing to do. I was working on all the hours.

We poured out the future together. Then it swarmed back in.

Little Everythings

I was stumbling toward wayward convergences
resembling marriages. I was assembled
of such tiny things I could hardly recognize myself.
It was all about structure and Seattle's gestures,
clouds gliding silently by on bicycles. I was on
a sad collection of streets, shuffling toward a room
nobody wanted. Stars hypothesized their shifting say.

There was no need for art but there it was.
Help with your hand fragments, clumsy as I was
about the latest war. I was settling in our house,
where everything was stolen and music echoed against the walls.
I created a false world, without promises, an abyss.
I swiveled my head here and there, dancing, then
sitting, then dancing, finally talking a great deal.

You were everywhere, leaving again, a miniature photograph
in the waving grass. I left myself with neighbors
who never mentioned it or returned me.
I will be invented, smaller, sluggish, without
speculation. I'll have a view in every direction
of the disappearing little roads and buildings, stretching
into nothing. I wanted someone to take my breath away.

Narrative of the Forgotten

Tiny centuries flick by at a lost window.
We arrive at the day of our undoing,

speech unleashed as clouds unlace their fingers.
Only the stark sky is left. *Pick the plumpest,*

he said. We met, both reaching for
the book of adjectives, tampering within

the body of the building that allowed small sentences.
I was ambivalent then, speculating on confessions.

The rose you gave me was cursive, loud,
without purpose. I was a sadness in your lonely

arrangement, losing what I never possessed. Is
the tale our destination? Is every form

an imaginary measurement? My drowning was
an apology for why the lake water

might change what was said.
You weren't ready. I am fragmentary gestures,

the difference between what can be seen
and what is known. My body begins questioning

objects containing no objections. I am
the glance at the water. I am perfectly broken.

Chlorophylled, Regenerative

I didn't. Then I did. The psychological rose
pinned on a green shirt that wore you inside out. Seams
showed. Insects spoke. Girls who knew you laughed,
diseased worlds that they were. I felt chewed, a lit language
uplifted within me. *Don't,* you said. *I'm a part of...*

I liked being fixed, slathered in the brightest silence.
You felt pale, smitten by weeds and ruined clouds
until grief snapped, defeating science. You weren't
sunlit by days, made of small moments.
I have learned to eat nothing or

I'm returned to that concealed world, where
you struggled with the opposable: broken glass;
green, curdled yogurt; crushed grass.
A flashlight in my face and I was all yours,
too many mouths on my skin. I burst.

Amateurs, or the Way I Like It

The attachments needed minor attachments
on either side of your neck. I thought
I could do everything myself; but the wires,
resonant near your mouth, called for help,
a familiar song. World news was wearing
sunglasses. Weather proclaimed a winner.
I could only tolerate something small. We fed
one another cables. I received messages.
Blame was reception. Signals hissed
safety procedures for starting again.

Our mistakes took us for a walk.
I was raining yet every part of me
was working. What did I know about
vestiges of time? They lived
in the very air we breathed. We looked
toward others and our knowledge to guide us.
So many transmissions were possible. Did we forget
to turn off the sad apparatus that startled us
with its terrible bird noise? At night we closed
our eyes, waiting for the appropriate adjustments.

Shy Instruments of Misunderstanding

Someone was suddenly behind you. Her hat,
her scandalous appetite for air, weren't extra-
terrestrial. Her bones poked through her skin.
You believed an apology was in order.

We were all tourists obfuscating empty space.
I entered, carrying *here* to *there,* and something became
attached to me. You described other places to be.
We stood at a window, smoke pressed into the evening.
(No different from anyone else).

You reached inside your companion, scooped out
something to comfort me. The moon scoured a table,
plucked an appetizer. You stood with your head on her
shoulder, getting technical. I explained the illusion
of setting your own house on fire.

Did you resemble me, surprised by a deficient afternoon,
limping scenery, our bodies with intentions of their own?
I had a question about all the small things that impeded us—
broken machines, objects skittering off table tops.
The world looked away from us just when we needed it the most.

PERSONAL CATASTROPHIC

Warn the Others

I desiccated letters, dispensed prescriptions, wrote strange, wandering lists. The inexplicable rushed into my sight, causing indecipherable utterances. I practiced the artist's life: becoming somebody else, a figment, a zigzag mind searching for an exit. I addressed everyone. My end increased exponentially. I followed my lack of logic and fell in love with ruined ideas. I consulted prehistoric thoughts like a dinosaur caught in a stranger's headlights. The startling lies, television, sex, food, drink—none of it mattered. I wanted what I wanted...

The wife within me was on her hands and knees, chiseling away at our evidence. Nothing was nourishing. We grew hungry and howled at irretrievable days. One list began:

speak to
countless cans
        of food
guns
        with small screams
at the end
                reckless days
        of aftermath
    fusillades of tongues

What I received:

abandoned galloping hair
    circling in wind
beautiful weeds
        in numb streets

I still want and more of me are coming.

Weather Left its Teeth Marks

Every dull moment has its resistance. Alive, a storm consumes itself, and wind scavenges the wreckage for insects and injury. I imitate bees that sting botanical lives, coughing up petals in their flight. My old self glued smiles on spoons and forks and ignored all those cold words. I was a mercenary whose sad password was *please*. Call my appearance what you want, my body is lost in its sideways suitcase.

Now I've collapsed and swarm with birds inside. My catastrophic fingers zigzag through air once filled with stars, pulling strands of my sacrificial hair. What to do with them? I isolate what's been broken and create a self-portrait. I'm afraid of the house, where sentences coagulate and everything occurs. Pets peel off in packs. Weather leaves a sample of a favorite day, the worried light. I live on less while asking for more. When I finish a gesture that means *Please don't hurt me,* I discover that even happy little books leave traces.

Syndrome: Circuitry of Eyes

The diagnosis is hypothetical,
birds and clouds picking and choosing,
unable to distinguish objects, a pear,
table, yellow eyes, leaf, claws. I was asleep
most of the time. The distance between
brick and sky grew mathematically.
My world was composed of edges
of awareness like steps startling at any sound.
Friends visited with little epilogues,
telling me it was the same everywhere.
I wanted to own air. I moved away from
myself, explained lapsing all around me.
I was dead in America and watching sunlight
diminish, become something else. Sky
was glad and broken. I was searching
for someone who could diagnose
our beautiful history, explain
what was pulling at my body and then
letting it go. I was shedding blood.
I had to get out and look
since they haven't told us yet
what to do about our symptoms.

Please, Me

The world is throwing out its voice matter-of-factly.
It means it. What's the use of a war
twice its size and running ahead? Fields

fill with shoes, ballooning with talk, stones,
bad wishes. Clouds crisscross to nowhere in particular.
We are revising as we speak. We are returning borrowed

thoughts, a last chance expiring. We are geographically
incorrect when a head explodes (one of a kind). Someone
is taking photographs, a bright wink in the abyss. Late

in the day our masculine ache fails, finds errors
everywhere. No beginning, no middle, no end. Unzipped,
we lift the bodies out; unzipped, I avoid someone's name.

Instruments are invited to what isn't finished. But the smell,
oh the smell. We grow closer to weight. A human symphony.
Take us with you and we promise a story about men, exploratory

dreams, ugly arguments, a plain door opening. Break a face,
borrow hollow limbs. Leave things halved. Release what's caught,
and, when you're done, put everything back into place.

The History of Animals That Arrived Late

Our bodies fail (with their historical abbreviations)
and we sweep them under a metaphorical rug.
I'm a little pile, the self that fell through myself.
Not the stranger squeezing sweet things out,
ending the way everything ends.

I'm outside. I'm leaving our kind.
The lopsided hold out longer, placing their feet
where we can see them. I count the ways
I've tried to leave my body behind. But my better parts
race into this new world of me in a mirror, me with
promontory crows, me in a gift hat from genealogical friends.

I'm the stranger who takes what I can,
praising the rest. I favor our anatomy,
our eyes target what's coming, our hearts resemble
biscuits. We cross the dark channel together,
raising our young on dreams that don't open, this new land
pushing us deeper into our past indecipherables.

The Color of Your Worry

Signs appeared everywhere.
There was nothing special in the way
our eyes' hardware closed to the swimming light.
All that space tried to surround us.
What more could I do? I couldn't see
outside of you (even plural you).

The devices meant to resemble our bodies
made you look extraordinary.
The bigger objects showed me
how our lives were accidental. I've torn
a leaf-shaped hole out of my inappropriate feelings
before offering them.

Some days I stumbled. I grew seeds
which confused themselves into becoming trees.
Which would you rather be? An angel or grass?
Clouds were upon me, with their
surprise maneuvers and string of sky.
I was agricultural, rising to the occasion.

What's this? Oh monster of mine.
            The moon, a curled body in a black bed.
            The whites of their eyes.
Tell me what you think we saw.

The Usual Meteorological Explanation

I look nothing like you.
A mouth, with its curious circuitry, unwinds
then returns, stapled to what lives inside.
We assembled all those adventures together;
commonplace as they were, they disappeared. Went where?
Intent, you say, *matters.* Intersecting.

None intended, I reply, inattentive to the horizon
in front of us, a placebo. I'm carried away
by the years spent on a red sofa waiting
for what might occur. I couldn't compare
to you, a body in its own world. Human,
ghost of what was once. I fly, become crispy.

Bits stick in my heart as I begin at the end.
I look like everyone else, another history
in the speck of an eye. You reciprocally thrive,
catch collapsing words between your teeth,
spit them out. I touch the flowers my mind
can't move, slipping over their frightened faces.

You can always think of us frolicking and happy.
You, with your incipient journeys and documents. You,
with your puppet-like tools. I'm mistaken for what
passes through the body, a day with its undone time,
its explosive praise. I'm another species
that believes everything happens for a reason.

Mistaken Selves in an Accident

The dog knew everything and I tried to forget him
until it was my turn. Black fur outside,
gravity inside. He counted birds,
in unusual arrangements. I took him into the woods,
which mistook me for someone else.

Creatures opened their throats like women persuading
us with words: *mysterious, wolves, weighty, arbitrary sky,*
inept shade. I was right about rancid leaves,
a woman screaming, her family buried deeply inside
one another. They mistook me for what they already said.

The dog knew what it wanted me to say.
We were interpreting the day differently,
its skittish light, a nothingness on the verge of empty.
The sad dog believed I was rain, or blowsy curtains,
or smiles that returned their teeth.

I shouted what I meant in another language,
using the vocabulary of those left behind.
I hoped someone would wake me like
a sparrow on a distant branch. How casual
we were with all that we had until the moment of impact.

Someone laughed. We were all wrong.

The Unexpected Invisible Woman

No romance. No feral organs. A thought unravels
against a spiritual landscape, which you can do without.
The woman kneels and was often found kneeling, confessing,
her former flesh smeared in first sunlight.

She's sentimental at your torn side. Pins and needles
invade your arm, the moon chews itself into nothing.
The one before her explained how
the body betrays itself.

At the beginning a page became beautiful, choosing
hours, until it, too, was transparent. The sound of hunger
is a withering balloon. Sun sleeps in the tiny face of a button.
The woman is dreaming of fauna.

Walls are meant to stop her dresses that don't
fit anymore. Every day different worlds shiver
in the cold. The woman, like rain, is continually asking
for something, lost in motion.

Here's your biblical town, filled with tragedy, infected and
mercenary. Wind wavers, calls. A neck snaps upward,
toward all that bright light, and people arrive as detectable
as happiness or another language.

The woman is a metaphysical disaster. Clouds urge
her bones to fly, form becomes shape and can't hold onto anything.
Accidents fall through her. She repeats what she knows until you return,
walk through her, mistaking her for the erratic weather.

A Theory for What Just Happened

Arrival came in the thought after
I did nothing for my body. The world was
leaning. The Survivalist knew it had come
to this, our hands filled with birds, too many insects
whirring on rooftops. He couldn't convince anyone.
He warned us about the way moonlight was galloping
here and there, sunsets embellishing themselves
in an alley. All those themes brought me closer to what
was next. Except for my belief in the bruises
that stumbled around my face. There was a time before this one
when we waited for the Survivalist to leave, his finger bones
leaving traces everywhere. Everything opening from the inside
out. Night was a parrot. Day smudged us. We told
our stories about the horizon without anything underneath it.
The moon couldn't stay still. I didn't want
to think about what would happen, trees like bullets.
My windshield clearly held one picture: someone's mouth
full of foreign air, someone else standing
on a gravel road with a yardstick in hand.
Havoc took me to the border of myself,
blew me a kiss, left me there.

Approximate

I was in the cave to change the things to be saved.
A girl was inside the story, then she was the story.
I had to study her before I moved her. Dark matter
smudged her face, her disinterested clothes,
undecided feet. I was an uninvited cloud to her sky.

I was there. I smoothed things over, wishing we had cars or
something to watch outside. But nothing could be changed.
My eye/her eye. Interchanged. She didn't want her body
anymore. She undressed. I had a mouthful of pretend bullets.
I grew lost. I didn't want to disturb her more than

she was already disturbed, having her clouds, then stories.
My eye usurped hers as I inspected her limbs. I couldn't save
dreams of rabbits or all the people I had known. I couldn't help
myself. Lost, I thought about the water outside drowning itself.
The sound it made.

We couldn't leave ourselves with our dangerous bodies.
We didn't know what lay beneath their surfaces.
I was filled with something cold. Her jellyfish skin.
I didn't know what to save first,
maybe her contagious echo.

The Most Stubborn Girl Escapes

I didn't know how to answer my body,
which swam past me, waving, then entered another country.

I wasn't as deep as I looked.

I drifted past someone's hands masquerading as eyes. I was too small
for the ghosts. Blue weather wept silently, softly,
covering its wrist of stars. I missed fields filled with strangers,
a face with a red mouth, my wasted life. I was beyond
laughing. I was crooked yet crying.
Heartbreak had already unknotted itself from my flesh,
scattered over stones the shape of a body.

Little nice things were breathing.

I shook something like sky so it wouldn't forget me.
I wanted to be loved the same way death changed everyone,
depending on the light. *Give me my body back.*
I'd accept a crack in my theory, a silly look, or the long grass
tickling me until I screamed. I left creaking things alone.
I needed the right audience. I found deciduous land,
a slender place, a disorder of trees filled with panicked birds.

I scrawled a neon question. My answer was nuclear.

Personal Catastrophic

1.

He lived where subtractions had reasons attached.
Equipped, open-mouthed, air flew from him. He couldn't hold
onto the buildings that crawled through poses before falling.
One echo stood over another, stood over... Sky was too late,
whittling itself into a villain. The world wasn't finished with him.
It was unanimous and becoming smaller. A day went missing.
Then another. He opened his box of wasted, important things,
removed his cat with her terrible fur, a sooty television,
his windows full of little insults. He was dangerously waiting.
Outside his feet swam in debris, kicking former architecture
in the preemptive light. No more borders to arrange, weeds fused
like gifts in a once-room.
      Dear you-are-not,
      Dearer pigeons and roads,
      Dearest empty weight,
Acknowledge what we have made but keep your hands for yourself.

2.

The trees, the bodies flew backwards, earth showed
its teeth. He was lulled by seawater rinsing his ankles.
Air translated into an old forgotten language. He wanted to scream
but couldn't. He wanted innocence not urgency.
He had fallen from the dark throat of a device.
He lost the recognizable landscape, a brutal missing.
He arrived or didn't arrive. Pieces gathered.
Rain stumbled across his face. A little bit of everything
flung itself at his feet, the world thoroughly unfixed,
rocks leaking blood. His mind dangled back and forth,
hurling, useless. He unbuckled his shoes, rose without them,
gathered what was left of his body. Nothing remained hidden.
Sky turned away, ribboning end to end. A foot in a shoe ran by.
The field with trees rose to meet him. No time to think
about all that water. He, too, draped himself on whatever
he could. Alive, somewhere, seeing what would happen next.

I Can't Get Away with Anything

My secret life wanted to explain things.
I didn't want to listen. It pushed me

further into spoiled weather, exhausted light,
that weird growth inside of me. I burned

your red shirt, burned the sunglasses
you used when you told me everything was fine.

Too much came out when they poked me.
They didn't know how to stop the feral memories.

Lightning was obviously diseased and replaced.
What they removed was sent to a forwarding address.

Parts of you go on and on, stopping
finally when a moment no longer listens.

I held you sideways, returned your fever to
your clothespin bones. The world's better this way,

the visible grass, the small pivoting plants reaching for what
they believed was light, tangled in too many explanations.

Irresistible Suicides

Somewhere the sea goes on and on.
Seeming is believing and I've stopped falling

like something smearing downwards,
colors with that faraway look, a bridge

I was meant to explain. Instead I pause,
poke my life with a stick. Nothing

is moving. Everything is yours now.
Don't cry. The world was like that:

the burned-out lights, empty sky, small betrayals.
My dreams threw me backwards.

I smile into my body, peeling it.
You could be family or not. I show you

it doesn't matter since I won't see you again.
I like the sound of ripping, breath at my neck,

clouds unraveling darkness. Somewhere,
in a boat, a woman is hurting herself and

I want to tell her to shut
everything behind her.

Nature Poem without Nature

We took other forms implied by our bodies,
unborn mice ghosting an abandoned town, small spines surfacing
in colorless fields, lurching involved with what
began to live. We were what we got ourselves into,
pieces of metal on a door. Silent propaganda
that was brutally indifferent.

                    Snow fell
and one of us was howling. He swallowed something
like sky. He leaned and no one would touch him.
We licked the dictionaries that were still in season.
We hadn't needed words in the riots of the early hours.
We'd forgotten the strangely familiar in our bewilderment.

         How trees could hold
nothing at all. How all that green withheld everything,
waiting for us to disappear. Nature was too close,
a charred bird in the hand was worth... Spoiled water
traveled incessantly over rocks like a condition. We wanted
property, a working hand. Opened, closed.

He Reminded Me of Me

Everyone held a piece of him and
the new world wouldn't let him out.
His pants and sweater contained certified parts.
A helping hand. Have a heart. The man arrived
on bone variations, a skin concerto. We took
what we could because nothing grew
in the fields and the earth passed him along.
We were made to obey. We sold the road
until it hurt. He was one of us. Or so
he said. He had complicated appetites,
eyeing a tragic woman, the lost and the blameless,
awkward instruments, substances from a mouth,
the sleep we were made from. Oh, breeze
creaking up my jointed legs, don't take that
immortal tone with me.
                         The road couldn't
tell us where to go with its absence of houses.
A two hundred year old light rose
from the bottom of a hill. That was when
he appeared all dog-legged and taunting.
What did he have that we couldn't remove from him?
Sky beat like a heart under a blue tee shirt,
we were happy and stabbed by light. We
walked together, he and I, losing things
like toes, feet, what rested inside of us.
We were islands, blood pooling, the structures
were anyone's guess. Small apologies fell
from trees, severed our concentration,
and took what they believed was rightfully theirs.

I Didn't Want to Know

Again the wolves were howling and we were hiding
in their fur. Light in the dark. Our eyes peeled for a first person
singular. Light glaring. And their bodies were broken televisions
filled with chromosomes, wandering limbs, oddly formed bones.

We were what was left, used up, prehistoric, stubbornly invisible.
The desolate landscape swallowed everything, weeds with
inexplicable hands, the scabby earth with scars and sudden
burials. Our pasts were too personal. Bats entered our world but

did nothing, their syllables impossible to hear. We weren't pretty,
the upholstery of our minds was overstuffed. We wanted to join them
there, where satellites fell through our heads. Light again. We knew to run.
A pause in the wind and we discussed the others, the argumentative or

detachable. We spoke too soon. For they grew all around us,
clicking. We smoothed skittish fur, stretched out sky's light.
We could see wicked trees with their windy voices. First light.
Their arms extended, telling us what we needed to live.

Post-Apocalyptic Etiquette

Introductions were congealing in the courtyard. He came
out of his house in metal clothes. We were shrubbery,
folding into our softer selves, enjoying windows.
He removed some cellophane but there was nothing

left in the package. He clattered here and there, turning
the moon round to see us with his meaty hands.
We kept our doubts and conceptions to ourselves.
Rocks argued among the bushes. Coffee water lulled

us to sleep. His grass was episodic, insects stubborn.
We turned another cheek if we had one. He laughed.
A couple struggled by under too much sky and
we wished for more of ourselves to greet them.

His mind wore surgical gloves that altered the dark shadows
of his address. Our worries said all the right things:
Put us in your enormous pocket or *These lights are too deliberate.*
We were looking for something we couldn't describe.

Everywhere a corner. His rickety heart was blown open.
We were full of nothing and wanted to be filled.
Bruised trees were politely bowing. Names were frail and
real. *Tin man,* we screamed at him. *Lion-hearted scarecrow.*

These Things Don't End Well

The children disappeared, unmended in my bones,
the room so inviting with its light flung into every corner.
All those hands in their plastic gloves. What drew my body
from its covering? I was torn. *Everything will be fine,*
if said enough, becomes a disease. Faces circled me
without mouths or noses. I wanted to jump off the table,
sing a loose assortment of scientific phrases. Outside
rain shredded air, pinning stray wings in trees.
I adjusted and adjusted.

     I climbed out of myself.
A head fell off after asking, *Who said too much?*
So much for animal desire. Others fled and arrived
at my bedside. Never have so many taken so little.
I was shrunken. Sunglasses stopped that light
from hurting me. I'd murmured, *Sorry,* and couldn't
seem to stop. The children were mute, misshapen,
waiting for daybreak. They promised to return.
But in the meantime anyone else would do.

STILL LIFE
WITH NERVOUS ANIMALS

One Sentence at Dinner

adapts to its surroundings,
losing itself in scattering fields or
tossed and falling against a slick, black dress.
The noun doesn't know itself well enough,
asks me to pass the beans.

How large the world is.
The noun exhales so loudly that birds explode from a bush
outside the window. I can't stop all the turning and
turning. A verb jumps in with contention.
Everyone sounds tinny.

What I was purported to say was stolen.
I disagreed with the noun, tried to translate.
All arguments are flexible and green, I tell
an adjective, seeking relief with wine.
A prepositional phrase sneaks off with slang.

I'm my own noise. A verb pockets
what it can and leaves. I tell how I've been
in a love letter. Once, when I was thinking about myself.
Even though the landscape I see now is open and intimate,
since then everything is less rhetorical than I remember.

I Couldn't Believe the Beautiful Lie

It was getting easier, all the little tongues
flapping their indulgences. This world argued every word,
breathing someone's story. I popped the rosette-shaped
thing between my teeth, swallowed, while birds
flew in my skylet, serrating clouds as I grew happier.

Nothing was fine for a while. My dreams wanted their mouths,
wanted me to wake up falling. I collected myself near fruit trees
armed with devices for the distraction of families.
A person could go crazy with chrysanthemums inside.
I welcomed the botanist, told him to find that

carnivorous flower, the one that liked me so much.
I suspected everyone's motives. It was hard to know my difference.
I had to take winged steps to know where I was going.
I had too much to say that didn't matter. These days
it was lie or be eaten, and I was wandering

under the strangest animal category. I wanted
to believe what every throat told me but I was too suspicious.
Every plant had its say, the dogs beside me waited
until I fell asleep. I wanted to jump in wholeheartedly
just to see what I could possibly do to the truth.

Somewhere, Too Long in the Sun

I didn't know where to put the minimal thoughts
that built up. I was repeatedly alone with bracelets
of grass against the ground. Parodies poured in
as though they were looking for help or objects of desire.
Couples smeared sunglasses against one another's eyes.
I was counting on their smiles, their senses of direction.
I could see where this was going. I would start over.
Whatever the dog thought he saw, he could only
remember the little things that moved
in a certain way. Was I so different? I was smarter
yesterday. I was sure the sky was turning toward evening
and whatever that had to say. Then sunlight surrounded me
like a beautiful girl. I asked her what I used to be like.
Water full of ideas, a tree with answers? People vanished
behind the moon, asked questions from cars, followed
a maze of paths, thinking. I remembered something
breathing too close to me, mumbling about time.

Calamitous and Teenaged

We ran into one, our house too small.
I was her invisible undergarment.

She was too much under construction, a child with
a mirror resembling everyone else,

a short disease with a youthful diagnosis.
A new haircut like rain.

I told her: never grow old, never become
a map of the body, roads leading every which way.

Her flesh and hair growled from aberrant green hats,
blue shirts, and aged pants.

Pieces of music emerged from the wrecked room,
unmistakable laughter. I had ears that carried me

through reenactments. I've found evidence,
a tattoo of a flamboyant tree, the nearest city translated

into a red dress, too much mouth. She didn't evaporate
or leave, becoming hair. I was tired. No more savvy

hunters and gatherers screaming outside our house. No more
cautionary tales to wake us up in the middle of the night.

I wanted to say that we were surrounded by streets
the shape of squares, that she smelled of leaves and wind

when she arrived late at our door. Our windows
were built of constellations. What to do with

stitches spreading across impatient questions?
Is this my life? Who was here first?

If only she were afraid.

Adorable, Unlikely, Nearly Figurative

She still wasn't reopened, even with all those electric sockets.
Whatever adorned her face, even as her newest version
described plenty. Some days we'd had enough and
couldn't fork through. We watched her finger
in a dog's mouth, his world swallowing,
answering incorrectly. Ah, for a rib cage instead of wings.
By the time we looked again, bees were on the radio,
ice catalogued human frailty, and she was bumping
glass as if it were the latest fashion.

What could we do that we hadn't done already? Pranks
inside the tiny houses, a little bit of religion waiting
as the last resort. We entered a cranial curve
and found ransom notes with lists of names.
She was prowling in moonlight for italics to wrap
her legs around. We understood. But we couldn't
do much, only hope for her metamorphosis into something
suitable, a dress or a hurricane or dreams leaking from a suitcase.
Since time was filling us all, then letting us loose.

I Am Born Lacking Emotional Content

Don't unbutton anything, the doctor's words
returned at this modern, lonely hour.
Ice cream, a man's shoes, and
a balcony disagreed. I swallowed
my luck like a myth unfolding into uncertainty,
juggled by a wind wrapping itself around
shy buildings. I adjusted, galloping
toward a place I wasn't invited.
When I became human the gods didn't know
what to do with their flexible hands. I stood
on concrete during special occasions, waiting
until it was late enough to adhere to a girl.
Some things evolved repeatedly, not me.
The girl drifted back to her untouchable mouth,
but she had less to say. I lacked photographs.
Had I come that far for nothing? I dreamed
that my shadow was stranded at the threshold.
I teetered. I organized myself into shapes:

A nostalgic stone;

Anthropomorphic hair;

An identified and interrupted boy.

I was beside myself while everyone
else was dependent, asking for help.
And all those tests proved nothing.

Eavesdropping Machine

The unborn divide themselves,
plot their migration. They expand
haphazardly. I'm flawed,
missing too many parts.

I can only hear limited speech,
my hands empty. I lift them toward
the sky with its suit of clouds. I wait for
the perfect conversation. I'm simple, approved

for takeoff in experimental weather. I'm here and
here and here like music. I believe in the invisible,
caught between feeling and the moment of
failure. I record wings and light, noise on

the surface of everything. The world becomes orchestral
as I break ancestral cogs, gears, wire, glass by mistake.
Large predatory words are used for thunder, sex, love,
death. I overhear sunrise and sunset and do what I'm asked.

Questions are volleyed between a man and a woman,
who seem familiar. Their utterances are unable to return
to their indiscreet mouths. A story unlike any other,
fragments, sentences breaking apart, measuring breath.

I'm close/not close. I'm contained/loosened.
Vocabulary can be unkind. I forget their bodies,
which vanish anyway. The man wants to say
something. I tell him: talk here >.
The unborn make sounds like remembering.

Where Do I Go From Here?

I was winning with all my nonsense;
my jangling mouth stormed my opponent's mind.
This was television, and her hero rose
into a newfangled sky.
A phantom answer hid inside me
abandoning noise, distance, and the hint of
owing anyone anything. I took her aside,
contesting one another. My question
donned sunglasses, tried to catch a plane.
I winced and couldn't explain the admirers
shuffling around with their personal memories.
I was on my own, no family or friends
with all their bandages and subtitles.
I was left with too much sky looking me
in the face. I didn't know what to do with her.
I wondered if she would die sooner or later.
I liked surprises. I liked debating the merits of...

Auction, or What We Thought They Were

One of my prettier selves hung in the basement. One of my thoughts couldn't contain itself so it returned to an available pile. There were too many inner breakings and beautiful devices beyond repair. Maybe a window would help with the forgettable scenery, take us out of ourselves. You loved the limping door, staccato notes from broken things. I tried to warn you how chairs made up their own minds, telling us too much.

We watched them leave all their instruments in places I liked to find them. I sat down. One of my musical selves wanted a conversation, where leaves were measured by sound.

I said that I wanted to bury a treasure, a collapsible adventure. They hardly had time to see me or my lovely silhouette. Nice as I was, I pulled apart the wings of ideas so they couldn't fly. My manipulative self laughed inside my practice room. Chairs couldn't sing although they tried, ugly professionals. They got what they asked for and I wasn't sure what that was.

Privilege

Oh, the fur in my face is storied with small recognitions. Names for everything bloom under a false white moon. I'll return, the next chance I get, to factories where workers worry in predictable ways, love their frivolous wives, chase days filled with nothing but forgetting what they're doing.

The tiny animal whispers into my soft places how I'm only allowed a certain kind of experience.

I'm inventing traditions that grow petulant while listening to world news wafting in wind. I'm broken by a happiness I can't recognize.

The tiny animal whispers into my soft places, vying for attention.

You don't need much, do you? Even now your sleekness, lack of a body, the way you cling at my neck. Between portrait and portraiture I remember something yearning to be something else. I am populated by what shines from electronic fever. I break things without emotional content.

The tiny animal whispers into my places that I am not soft.

One helps the other. Festering begins inside the animal I worship. We are alone. I kiss a form like mine but without accoutrements as I watch steel being bent into fashionable clothes. We are all asking to be taken apart, redistributed.

Set This House on Fire

They tried to convince you to discuss your complications, not
happiness exactly, your man-made future. You were given a moment...
then another. Sky asked who could do what to whom? You were among
parenthetical trees at the time of night everything was whittled down to
nothing. Birds understood eviction. Insects knew that sidewalks scorned
your feet in sunlight. Evening slowly rearranged fields, and homes grew
nervous. You thought about anger, and the bedrooms went first, then
a bathroom, a ghost limb. The showy flowers lit up in the darkness.
You smelled gasoline, sulfur, mint. Windless sounds surrounded you.
The empty house dined on your breath.

Exhibit A: blinking flames, stars burned to nothing.
Exhibit B: speak for yourself, air fleeing.
Exhibit C: cut and folded, everything along the lines.
Exhibit D: a match raised with further complications.

Give Me Extravagant Lights

I'm simmered to nothing,
luminous incantations, words
larger than clots of color. Vegas,

with sun embedded between its missing fingers.
Silent pharmaceutical fragments.

I pretend astonishment. I feel your adept
holes, try to replace them. I can't find
what you're looking for when it's a whistle/

prairie grass/full sentences/ the bodiless moon.
I get lost in the process. There's
an unfavorable inspection of hands and

I take comfort because everything is mine.
A little bit of the sky is wasted on me.

Lights surround us as if to say, *you don't have
to take this*. I ask about the big picture and
you reply, *It shows itself to everyone else but you.*

Bone Sampler

A world ago a word startled the animals. Small intervals reigned.
I crawled out from secrets in a basement into something wrong.
I breathed that *no,* gathered longing, hunted emphasis.

I made this town look bigger, its echo growing flamboyantly over
cars and houses that confessed to nothing. Those days were long gone,
the ones that explained my nerves and the way I pulled myself from the
wreck of myself.

I tried to name each cell muscled into being. I tried to be a fish inside
my cat's brain. Out of all the questions still left unanswered is the one
about luck. In the end a melodramatic sun slips out of our hands and
shatters against wrinkled water and what's left is the mere skeleton
of that original sentence.

An Autobiographical Moment with a Moth

I held biographic wings in my hand.
Scientific, I was thinking about
conversations and the spaces they left.
For some there was the rest.
For others, we understood
the diagnostic part of the happy world. I wandered,
taking my things, equipment that repeated itself,
my temporary home, beauty that unfolded,
calling everything inside, something unnoticeable
to lay antennae against. The moth wore all it owned,
a miniature cloud. I tasted light, wanting
an adjective. I waited for a point,
but the two of us were slowly breaking.
Illusion unexpectedly flapped the shrubs.
I was waiting for a misanthrope to arrive,
stumbling by trees and rocks, bursting through leaves or
flowers until darkness pinched off our heads.
Moonlight reassured me. I hated it
when we smiled. I was used to things happening
without me. I watched the moon begin to float.
At times like this I understood that nothing was made for me.
But that didn't mean it couldn't be explained.

Still Life with Nervous Animals

Too much was stolen that day to change
his mind. What grew on the goats stayed on
the goats as he fell into himself.
The revolution was flattered, talking into a microphone
that resembled a human body. Misery assembled
with a peculiar silence, diseased and searching
through his childhood. But it was the years afterwards
that he meant to explain, how a certain dream
sang to him, then flew away. He wanted the shivering sheep
to keep to themselves, not to wander toward

wobbling drapes the color of his incredulous arms. Streets
beyond his window offered refractable light.
What could beauty or politics do with him except identify
hands and legs? He was crawling, dragging
what he could from the explosion that confused
everything, interrupted the flies. He was burning
with something he called perfection. He would create
what he could in that country filled with mistakes
and contradictory instructions. He would paint notable
animals from somewhere else. The kangaroos were waiting.

Exponentially Yours

Some things go on and on with little encouragement:
a seizure of water, the bird-flavored sky, a cell dividing.
It was crowded there, clean, white, and stunned.
I liked on and off switches attached to things.
I wanted to arrive at my destination the way
everything broken moved into an adjoining space.
Too many of my selves were caught in a mirror.

I met myself again, one foot following another
like a romance. *Multiply,* I ordered. I needed to investigate,
offer what I hadn't acquired yet. Too many pieces surfaced,
wanting reassurance. I could find popular belief
everywhere. I was an ordinary reoccurrence caught
in a moment that continued. My mind argued, won,
and still lost. I wasn't trying hard enough.
I wasn't trying at all. Yet I couldn't imagine stopping.
I couldn't be brief in my whereabouts.

In My Right Hand: Everything Left

Once again my fingers were visiting
before the rain of animals. I only wanted
to talk. That love was indifferent,
its wife asleep. I didn't know how to leave
or stop saying, *It's hard to know what you have.*

I could point at what I wanted, shout,
ready, set, go, after something, but what?
That dark, little self? The season's repeated
compulsions? Eyes unable to repel the curious,
I held onto my courteous little animals.
Over there a vending machine had choices
and air its various versions of abandonment.

I am my own landscape, seen from
a lazy distance. I will learn to juggle
a scene, field, cloud, tree, morning.
I look out the moving window, wave
at whatever's looking and whatever's not,

hoping nothing there will tear me apart.

This Could Be a Solution

since it's not a black dress, designed for a quandary.
I was deferential as you introduced your missing unhappiness,
with its riddles and positions between random clouds.
We were bereaved, bristling in the blonde grass, waiting for
our feet to practice tiny acts of violence.

Version 7

We were full of historical errors that couldn't come around to
our way of thinking about augmentation or how a shirt
wrapped itself around an object. Leave the hem as you would
someone drowning. Leave the dark sleeves hidden.

Version 20

More of what has happened wasn't a solution because
it interrupted the hours. You weren't sleeping
without your ideas, were you? My mind was silent,
as though full of everything, along with black shoes.

Version 36

Yesterday the happiest spot was near your knees.
You were dancing to make the music louder, rhyming in all
that empty space. Watch it fly toward the rising surface.
We have to be careful where we move our feet. Hazardous
floors, querulous questions, and chairs surround us.
You could lose yourself in permeable folds.

Version 52

Between more than us, sky was stuttering with a disguised you.
All that music was friendly, so you could offer your good
hand, the one that didn't lie or say it was something it wasn't.
Like a beginning. Like some magical machine.
I was careful where I kept my body.

Version 64

I was sorry that it was what it was. The solution looked better
in blue. All that blonde grass was an announcement.
Things could fall, trees becoming furniture
with limitations. I've learned to hate the edges,
stairs, homes, sentences. I'm growing carefully unconscious.
All those black dresses will find us. I want them to use us
so they can dance in small, wistful towns. What is draped
is opening, as though it's everything flushed from the answer.

Acknowledgments

Grateful acknowledgment is made to the following publications in which these poems appeared, some in earlier versions.

Colorado Review: "Still Life with Nervous Animals"

Connotation Press: "Personal Catastrophic," "Approximate," "How Are You, Hypothetically?"

Denver Quarterly: "Learning a Thing or Two," "I Am That Thing," "I Can't Get Away with Anything" (formerly "Making Sense"), "Anonymous," "Where Do I Go From Here?"

Eunoia Review: "Syndrome: Circuitry of Eyes"

Final State Press: "Privilege"

The Journal: "Love Poem with Too Many Distractions," "Nature Poem without Nature"

Misfit Magazine: "A Day of Nothing Else," "Warn the Others," "Target Practice," "I Am Born Lacking Emotional Content," "The Unexpected Invisible Woman," "Irresistible Suicides," "Eavesdropping Machine"

New World Writing: "Shy Instruments of Misunderstanding," "Chlorophylled, Regenerative," "This Could Be a Solution," "As Things Fell Down"

Poetry Northwest: "In My Right Hand: Everything Left"

Salamander: "Pillow"

Superstition Review: "Calamitous and Teenaged," "A Crack in Everything Else"

Verse: "A Theory for What Just Happened," "Post-Apocalyptic Etiquette," "I Didn't Want to Know," "He Reminded Me of Me," "Please, Me"

About FutureCycle Press

FutureCycle Press is dedicated to publishing lasting English-language poetry in both print-on-demand and Kindle (eBook) formats. Founded in 2007 by long-time independent editor/publishers and partners Diane Kistner and Robert S. King, the press incorporated as a nonprofit in 2012. A number of our editors are distinguished poets and writers in their own right, and we have been actively involved in the small press movement going back to the early seventies.

We award the FutureCycle Poetry Book Prize and honorarium annually for the best full-length volume of poetry we published that year. Introduced in 2013, proceeds from our Good Works projects are donated to charity. Our Selected Poems series highlights contemporary poets with a substantial body of work to their credit; with this series we strive to resurrect work that has had limited distribution and is now out of print.

We are dedicated to giving all of the authors we publish the care their work deserves, offering a catalog of the most diverse and distinguished work possible, and paying forward any earnings to fund more great books. All of our books are kept "alive" and available unless and until an author requests a title be taken out of print.

We've learned a few things about independent publishing over the years. We've also evolved a unique and resilient publishing model that allows us to focus mainly on vetting and preserving for posterity poetry collections of exceptional quality without becoming overwhelmed with bookkeeping and mailing, fundraising activities, or taxing editorial and production "bubbles." To find out more about what we are doing, come see us at www.futurecycle.org.

The FutureCycle Poetry Book Prize

All full-length volumes of poetry published by FutureCycle Press in a given calendar year are considered for the annual FutureCycle Poetry Book Prize. This allows us to consider each submission on its own merits, outside of the context of a traditional contest. Too, the judges see the finished book, which will have benefitted from the beautiful book design and strong editorial gloss we are famous for.

The book ranked the best in judging is announced as the prize-winner in the subsequent year. There is no fixed monetary award; instead, the winning poet receives an honorarium of 20% of the total net royalties from all poetry books and chapbooks the press sold online in the year the winning book was published. The winner is also accorded the honor of being on the panel of judges for the next year's competition; all judges receive copies of all contending books to keep for their personal library.

www.ingramcontent.com/pod-product-compliance
Lightning Source LLC
Chambersburg PA
CBHW070011100426
42741CB00012B/3199